COVENANT • BIBLE • STUDIES

When God Calls

Mary Jessup

faithQuest® ♦ Brethren Press®

Covenant Bible Studies Series

Copyright © by *faithQuest*®. Published by Brethren Press®, 1451 Dundee
Avenue, Elgin, IL 60120

Cover photo: D. Jeanene Tiner

01 00 99 98 97   5 4 3 2 1

Library of Congress Cataloging-in-Publication Data
Jessup, Mary, 1950–
    When God calls / Mary Jessup.
        p. cm. —(Covenant Bible studies)
    ISBN 0-87178-009-7 (pbk. : alk. paper)
    1. Bible—Biography—Study and teaching. 2. Vocation—Biblical
    teaching—Study and teaching. I. Title. II. Series: Covenant
    BS605.2.J47 1997
    220.9'2'071—dc21   97-6389

Manufactured in the United States of America

Contents

Foreword

The Covenant Bible Studies Series was first developed for a denominational program in the Church of the Brethren and the Christian Church (Disciples of Christ). This program, called People of the Covenant, was founded on the concept of relational Bible study and has been adopted by several other denominations and small groups who want to study the Bible in a community rather than alone.

Certain characteristics make relational Bible study unique. For example, it is anchored in covenantal history. God covenanted with people in Old Testament history, established a new covenant in Jesus Christ, and covenants with the church today. Therefore, relational Bible study is intended for small groups of people who can meet face-to-face on a regular basis and share frankly with a group that has covenanted for mutual accountability and encouragement.

Relational Bible study, then, takes seriously a corporate faith. As each person contributes to study, prayer, and work, the group becomes the real body of Christ. Each one's contribution is needed and important. "For just as the body is one and has many members, and all the members of the body, though many, are one body, so it is with Christ. . . . Now you are the body of Christ and individually members of it" (1 Cor. 12:12, 27).

Relational Bible study helps individuals and the group to claim the promise of the Spirit and the working of the Spirit. As one person testified, "In our commitment to one another and in our sharing, something happened. We were woven together in love by the Master Weaver. It is something that can happen only when two or three or seven gather in God's name, and we know the promise of God's presence in our lives."

The burlap cross, with its interwoven threads, the uniqueness of each strand, the unrefined fabric, and the rough texture, characterize covenant groups. The people in the groups are unique but interrelated; they are imperfect and unpolished, but loving and supportive. These divergent threads create the shape of the cross, the symbol for all Christians of the resurrection and presence with us of Christ our Savior. Like the burlap cross, we are brought together, simple and ordinary, to be sent out again in all directions to be in the world.

Here are some guidelines that will help create an atmosphere of deepening faith and support in your group:

1. As a small group of learners, simply gather around God's word to discern its meaning for today. Let the words, stories, and admonitions you find in scripture come alive to challenge and renew you in their practical applications to daily life.
2. Remember that all people are learners and all are leaders. Learn from one another, and take responsibility for offering guidance and encouragement, as appropriate. In this way, each person will contribute to the study, sharing the meaning found in the scripture and helping to bring meaning to others.
3. Recognize each other's vulnerability as you share out of your own experiences. For in sharing we learn to trust others and to be trustworthy.

Additional suggestions for study and group-building are provided in the "Sharing and Prayer" section. Use them in the hour preceding the Bible study to foster intimacy in the group and to relate personal sharing to the Bible study topic.

Finally—welcome to this study! As you search the scriptures, may you also search yourself. May God's voice and guidance and the love and encouragement of brothers and sisters in Christ challenge you to live more fully the abundant life God promises.

Preface

The Greek word for church, *ekklesia*, means "the called out ones." As members of Christ's church, we need to listen for ways in which God calls us to do the work of ministry. The church also needs to be aware of its role as the body of Christ, charged with calling men and women to do God's work. Calling is not just a privilege for the select few. It is an invitation to all of us to use our gifts in service to God.

This study, *When God Calls*, explores the lives of different biblical characters, looking at the variety of ways that God called them to do important work for the world. As we explore our own calls, we'll look at different rituals of our churches that discipline us for a life of service. Many of our practices, such as the Lord's Supper, baptism, ordination, and the laying on of hands, remind us that we have been called by God.

During this study, keep in mind the ways in which God has called you, and open yourself to the possibility that God is still calling you. Be aware, as well, of initiatives your congregation can take on behalf of Jesus Christ to call out the talents and gifts of its members.

Recommended Resources

By the Manner of Their Living (20 min. video). Brethren Press. Stories of how Brethren respond to God's call upon their lives through their work, lifestyle, and witness. Available for rent or purchase.

Exploring the Call to Ministry (20 min. video). Brethren Press, 1991. Interviews of little children and practicing pastors who share their views of ministers and ministry. Available for purchase.

Ministry manuals and books of worship for your denomination; videos and other denominational resources related to call.

Bowman, John David. *Invitation to the Journey*. Brethren Press, 1990. Addresses membership issues and provides suggestions for revitalizing commitment to Christ through a more meaningful understanding of church membership.

Buswell, Sara. *Here Am I: Responding to God's Call*. Baker Book House, 1989. A look at the God who calls, ten biblical characters who responded to call, and Jesus' response as an example for our own response.

Monkres, Peter. *We Follow Christ.* Christian Board of Publication, 1989. A study on being called in today's world. Broad themes include the one who calls; the commitment to the call; and the many implications of following Christ in family life, through vocation, in relation to the nation, the church, and the world.

Nouwen, Henri J. M. *The Road to Daybreak: A Spiritual Journey.* Doubleday, 1988. A deeply personal sharing that will call readers to new awareness of God's call in their own lives.

1

God Calls Abraham
Genesis 12:1-9

God initiates the call of Abraham and Abraham responds in faith. Today we reenact this attitude of graciously accepting God's call every time we participate in the Lord's Supper, where we partake of that which is freely given.

Personal Preparation

1. Read Genesis 12:1-9 and reflect on Abraham's call. If you had been Abraham, how might you have responded?
2. Review your phone bills for the last few months. Do you tend to make more calls or receive more calls?
3. Think about how your congregation celebrates the Lord's Supper. What aspect of the service is the most meaningful for you? Why?

Understanding

This whole notion of call and response is a broad and often elusive topic. One of the most helpful things we can do is narrow the focus and look at different elements each week. We'll begin by centering on the one who is doing the calling. It is God who initiates the process. God often works through angels, people, or burning bushes—but always God does the calling.

So often, when Christians meet to talk about call and their response to it, they focus on the respondent rather than the initiator. One look at our monthly telephone bill will convince us of the centrality of the one initiating the call. In our biblical discussions, too, we must identify the initiator of the call and the respondent to the call. They are not one and the same. We don't call ourselves.

God calls! That's really quite amazing. God calls people like us and chooses to work through us. If I were God and needed something done, I'm not sure I'd go through the hassle of calling a human to do my work. Eleven years as a pastor taught me that "if you want something done on time and meeting your expectations, do it yourself." It's a terrible administrative style. You do everything from scouring the kitchen sink to serving as your own worship leader, and you're always alone. But it gets done. You get tired and burned out, but it gets done the way you want it to get done. It seems that God, however, who loves union and communion, prefers not to work alone. Instead, God calls people like you and me to an amazing variety of kingdom tasks. On those days when my husband washes the dishes, I have a hard time. I prefer the correct method of stacking dishes in the drainer: "the vertical stack method." It gets a bit precarious, because all of the dishes must end up in the drainer. He, however, uses a horizontal method. Dishes only go into the drainer if they fit neatly. The rest he strings up and down the kitchen counter, which leaves the entire kitchen looking like a disaster zone. I'd rather wash them myself. Then they would be done my way—the right way.

God surely has incredible patience to work through human beings. But that seems to be the way God works. We must keep this foremost in mind. God initiates the calling process and God calls us to certain tasks. We're so accustomed to keeping the focus upon ourselves that when we talk about calling, we forget God and talk instead only about our role in responding. But from Abraham we learn that the wonder isn't so much that we say yes to God's call but that the call was ever extended in the first place.

The language common to many churches is so self-centered: "I've accepted Jesus." Maybe the bigger deal is: "I've *been accepted* by Jesus!" The first statement makes it sound as though we've done Jesus a favor by taking him in; the other sounds more like the acknowledgment of a gift. A gift is exactly what call is all about. Sure, it's a task, but first it is a gift, a gift we did not request.

When my denomination's conference theme was "Living in Obedience to God's Calling," we heard a lot about the obedience part and less about God's part. Living in obedience is a task, but the call is a gift, unearned and unexpected. And we can't cultivate an "attitude of gratitude" when all we think about is the work required from us.

All of this tells us why God's call to Abraham is a good place for our discussion to start. The first eleven chapters of the Bible are universal in scope. But, as we are introduced to Abram in the later verses of chapter 11, the focus shifts to the story of this one particular person. He is married to Sarai, who has been unable to bear children. We learn that Abram is a son of Terah, a descendant of Shem, Noah's son (Gen. 11:27-31). Terah's family is from Ur of the Chaldeans. It was Terah who left Ur and took his son, Abram (and Abram's wife, Sarai, and his grandson, Lot), and headed for the land of Canaan. But when they got to Haran, they settled there. And in Haran Terah died.

God's call of Abram comes in chapter 12. We're not told why God chose

Abram; no description of the man tells of any unusual characteristics he might have possessed. We're simply told that the Lord said to Abram, "Go . . . ," and he went (v. 4). In accounts of call that we'll consider later, God's victims objected or asked for clarification. But not Abram.

From this account we almost sense that the future of Abram and Sarai is predetermined. They are getting older and have no children. We get the idea that their nephew Lot will play a significant role in this story; he'll probably receive the inheritance. Yet God makes promises to Abram. They include a land and a great nation of his descendants who will play a significant role in the history of salvation. "So Abram went, as the Lord had told him" (v. 4). They headed for Canaan.

The call to leave things behind, to head off for the unknown, is a common theme in stories of calling. In Abram's case the land was occupied: "Canaanites were in the land." A call often leads us into a frightening situation. But in this context, Abram responds by building an altar to the Lord and calling on the name of the Lord. This becomes a recurring pattern in the Abram story. He often builds an altar to commune with his God.

The writer of Hebrews uses Abraham as an example of faith. "By faith Abraham obeyed when he was called to set out for a place that he was to receive as an inheritance; and he set out, not knowing where he was going" (Heb. 11:8). We applaud this man as a hero of the faith, because of his risky response to God's call; but Abraham would probably encourage us to take the focus off of his response and look instead at the initiator of the call.

God not only called Abraham, but God was Abraham's provider and sustainer. The first three verses of chapter 12 tell us that Abram was to go, and then we're told what God's work would entail. Look at all the "I wills": "I will show . . . I will make . . . I will bless . . . I will curse." It's clear that God is the primary actor on this stage.

The initial call to Abram conveys several promises, though they are sketchy in nature. But as we follow the story of Abram, we find additional encounters with God whereby the call expands. Each of the further revelations, however, refers to the initial promises. God will be faithful to those promises. Abram believes this.

Maybe building an altar to the Lord served to remind Abram of the covenant he had with God. The word *religion*—"back again" (*re*) and "to bind" (*ligio*)—means to re-focus, re-center, re-align, re-mind. People who have experienced a call from God need ways in their religious life to be reminded of that initial call. Abram built altars. We, as Christians, also remind ourselves of the God who calls. In our tradition it is the Eucharist, or the Lord's Supper, the bread and the cup, that calls us to remember. Jesus said, "Do this in remembrance of me" (1 Cor. 11:24). Without such remembrances we risk forgetting our religion.

Through symbols we visually express what is verbally inexpressible. By taking the bread and eating it and by lifting the cup and drinking it, we proclaim the Lord's death until he comes. It is an act. It is an aid to help us remember. Through this, we are called to remember the one who initiated the call to us. At the Lord's table, we experience in a profound way that God is in charge and that we are responding to an invitation that God extends to us in grace.

Walter Brueggemann writes: "All key words of the Lord's Supper drama have Jesus as subject and not us. We are the subject of no important active verbs. At the table Jesus took. He blessed. He broke. He gave to us again. It's his table. We're guests. We don't fix the menu or pay the bill." And yet in many churches, when the invitation to the table is extended, the focus is often on the unworthiness of the partaker rather than on the grace of the initiator.

 We need to be re-bound. We need religion. God calls. Like Abram, we need to respond with gratitude that God calls even us.

Discussion and Action

1. In what instances have you felt God calling you? How did you know it was God?
2. Why did God pick Abram? What if Abram had said no?
3. Do we have any role in determining whether God will call us? Discuss what that might be.
4. Why do you think God chooses to work through humans?
5. The Lord's Supper is one way to express gratitude for God's call to us. Share some of your experiences related to the Lord's Supper. How has its meaning grown and/or changed for you?
6. What are some other ways to express gratitude for God's calling? Covenant with one other person about a way you will express your gratitude to God this week.

2

God Calls Moses
Exodus 2:23—3:12

God heard the cries of the Israelites suffering under their Egyptian slave masters. Who would deliver them? Our baptism identifies us as God's beloved, called to respond to the cries God hears today. But we must overcome our natural reluctance and push aside unworthy excuses.

Personal Preparation

1. Carefully read Exodus 2:23—3:12, and then recall your baptism. How did you perceive God's call to you on that day?
2. Reflect on the call of Moses, his early life in Egypt, his flight to the wilderness, his actual experience of being called. Why would God call a person who was shy and had a speech impediment? When have you seen "weaknesses" becoming strengths through God's power?
3. Read through the hymn "Sing, Child of God" (p. 54). What themes in this song are most meaningful to you?

Understanding

When we're introduced to Moses in this passage, we find that he is married, has a child, and works for his father-in-law. As a shepherd in the wilderness, Moses' life is probably quite routine. But all that is about to change. He is about to be called by God.

Moses is far away from the place of his birth. Although an Israelite, Moses was raised in the home of an Egyptian pharaoh's daughter. All the while, he maintained his identity as an Israelite, and as he grew older he grew in compassion for his people. One day when he saw an Egyptian beating a Hebrew, Moses stepped in, killed the Egyptian, and then hid the body. He felt justified in defending a fellow Hebrew and assumed other Israelites would approve as well. But they didn't share his sense of justice. Then, when Pharaoh heard of the crime, he sought to kill Moses and Moses fled to the faraway land of Midian. He probably resigned himself to living in exile for the rest of his life. But God had other plans.

God, too, had perceived the needs of the people of Israel, having heard their cries for help. Remembering the promises made to Abraham, God begins to work. The plan involves Moses.

Have you noticed the similarities between God and Moses in this story? Both have seen the affliction of their people and choose to respond in some way. Moses' way is unacceptable, because violence and murder are no solution. God's plan is to use this man Moses in better ways.

Moses encounters the revelation of God in the spectacular flames of a burning bush. The bush is on fire but the fire does not consume it. Moses reacts with attraction and repulsion, curiosity and fear, as God proclaims the ground holy and declares: "I am the God of your father, the God of Abraham, the God of Isaac, and the God of Jacob" (Exod. 3:6). Then God becomes specific about the purpose of this strange encounter: it is a call to action! Moses must go to Pharaoh to arrange for the release of the Hebrews from slavery.

Moses begins to object. "Who am I that I should go to Pharaoh, and bring the Israelites out of Egypt?" (v. 11). Moses clearly does not believe himself qualified for the task. Later Moses pleads, "I have never been eloquent . . . I am slow of speech and slow of tongue" (4:10). Yet with Moses' every objection, God counters with a promise to be present.

Was Moses a gifted guy who was truly humble, or was he indeed a poor choice? He seems quite different from Abram, for we have no evidence that Abram questioned God's call. Moses, on the other hand, is definitely reluctant to agree to God's plan for him. It seems that Moses is quite aware of the monumental nature of the task to which God is calling him. Maybe he has a good, objective understanding of his personal limitations. Yet God won't take no for an answer, responding only with words of assurance.

It makes me wonder, Does God always match up our obvious gifts with our call? When serving my local church as the on-site coordinator for a district conference, I first consulted with the pastor and a respected lay leader in putting together a committee. Then I asked eighteen individuals to coordinate various areas of responsibility. I tried to match up the gifts of the people with the tasks at hand as in 1 Corinthians 12, where Paul writes about varieties of gifts used for the common good. But if we can trust Moses' self-assessment, this story seems to tell us that we are sometimes called to a task that will stretch our gifts and natural inclinations to the maximum. Moses was not a gifted speaker and we're given no evidence that he ever became one. But he did become a gifted administrator, and his brother Aaron served as his spokesman.

The cries of the people of Israel suffering in slavery are heard by their God, and God is going to deliver them. Moses is God's choice for a leader. Excuses fall by the wayside. There is work to do.

Instead of being an adopted son in Pharaoh's royal family, he becomes Moses, the leader of the Hebrews. He now has a new identity. And it all started with a groan and a cry. One way the church helps us understand our identity is through baptism. Here's how William Willimon, a United Methodist writer, puts it: "The principal, primal, initiating, continuing way I experience my identity as a Christian is in baptism. The more the baptized learn to see their whole life in the light of their baptism, the more does their life take on the pattern of life in Christ."

In the synoptic Gospels we read that as Jesus came up out of the water at his baptism, a voice came from heaven saying, "This is my Son, the Beloved, with whom I am well pleased." It was at his baptism that Jesus received his vocation, his peculiar destiny, his identity. Jesus' baptism answered the question, "Who is this one?" God gave the answer: "He is my beloved Son." And our baptism answers the identity question for each of us, moving hymn writer Lena Willoughby to exult . . .

Sing, child of God, to a weary world;
Sing of your faith, let its joy be unfurled. . . .
Sing, child of God,
Sing, share, and rejoice!

Yes, we are God's children, and this marvelous truth is cause for rejoicing. Just as water was broken at our birth and a name given to us, so too at our baptism we come from the water and are claimed by God.

What does it mean to be called, to be named a child of God? God tells Moses to say to Pharaoh, "Thus says the Lord: Israel is my firstborn son . . . . Let my son go that he may worship me" (4:23). God has plans for the firstborn. They are to serve. Old Testament scholar Walter Brueggemann writes in *Living Toward a Vision:* "God says to Pharaoh, 'Israel is not a slave. Israel is my son. Take another look. My son is not a brick layer. My son is destined for something that can't possibly happen in your regime, Pharaoh.' "

A child of God is called to serve. With ears that hear as God hears, we can pick up the distress signals that surround us. Later, we'll look at the call of the disciples and see that it was Jesus' compassion for harassed and helpless people that led to the call of the twelve (Matt. 9:35-37). God calls us not just to give each child a little something to do, but God calls us in response to a real need. Moses was called because the people of Israel were in slavery. Jesus' disciples are called because there are some needy people who need the gospel.

Let us think of our baptism, then, when we think of our call, because the waters of baptism symbolize cleansing. To perceive the needs around us, we must have eyes that see and ears that hear, and so often our eyes and ears must be flushed with cleansing water. There is no shortage of misery to which God responds. So to be called is not all there is; we are called *to* something. The real issue is whether or not we are tuned in to the call and to the cries for help. The nonverbal call of God and the sometimes deafening cry of humanity are inextricably linked. Our baptism claims us as God's beloved. As God's beloved we are called to respond as God responds.

Again, William Willimon helps us here, as he tells this story of Martin Luther: "When old Luther was suffering from self-doubt or despair, wandering through some dark night of the soul and sailing inkwells at the devil, he received great comfort by touching his forehead and saying '*Baptismus sum* . . . I am baptized.' Remembrance of his baptism brought comfort and assurances, because, said Luther, our God is a jealous God who does not willingly share that which he owns, and baptism is a perpetual sign that God owns me."

We often focus on who *we really ought to be* and lose sight of who, by God's grace, *we already are.* Living by faith is always more about what God does for us than what we do for God. As baptized, beloved children of God, we are called to respond to the needs around us. It is the way God worked with Moses. It is the way God works with us.

Discussion and Action

1. Share together about your experiences of baptism. From your thinking in preparation for this lesson, tell about any perceptions of God's call on the day of your baptism. What difference does baptism make to the way we respond to God's calling? How is your baptism still a reminder of God's call?

2. What is your experience of a personal "weakness" becoming a strength with God's help? (Refer to the Apostle Paul's statement about this in 2 Corinthians 12:7-10.)

3. In your opinion, did Moses' objections to God's call come from true humility or from fear or pride? What have been some of your own objections to God's call in the past?

4. From your experience and/or observation, would you say that God always matches up our gifts with our call? Or does God call us to tasks that, as the author states, "stretch our gifts and natural inclinations to the maximum"? Explain.

5. How do you deal with your limitations when you're called to something difficult? Who is your Aaron? How can the church encourage

Moses/Aaron relationships?

6. What are some of the needs around you that God might call a Moses to address? For example, if God called you to run for the local school board, how would you respond?

7. How does God respond to the cries of people and work to alleviate suffering today? Brainstorm for some ways your covenant group could respond.

3

God Calls Samuel and Hannah
1 Samuel 3:1-21

Even before his birth, Samuel was consecrated for the work of God by his mother, Hannah. In consecrating our children, we acknowledge the need to nurture them in the faith—that they, too, might hear the call of God.

Personal Preparation

1. Who nurtured you in the faith, causing you to grow in Christian faith and commitment today? Whom have you been able to nurture in this way?
2. Read 1 Samuel 3:1-21. Reflect on any call experiences you had as a child or youth. What can you share with your group about such a call?
3. Compare Hannah and Samuel's story to Mary and Jesus' story in Luke 2. How are the stories alike? What were the two mothers called to do?

Understanding

God's call to Samuel is only one part of this lesson. It also focuses on God's call to Samuel's parents and teacher, a call to rear the child to be God's servant. In chapter one, we learn that Samuel is the child of Hannah, one of several barren women in the Bible who were blessed with children late in life. Hannah prayed to God for a son, promising that she would give her child back to God. God answered Hannah's prayer. So grateful was she that she dedicated her son to God even before he was born. Then when Samuel was weaned, Hannah took him to the house of the Lord in Shiloh and gave him to Eli, the priest.

Eli and Samuel are constant companions. The priest guides Samuel in his education, and the devoted boy guides the old man whose eyesight has failed him. They are indispensable to each other. In this loving environment, Samuel grows "both in stature and in favor with the Lord and with the people" (2:26).

God called to Samuel when he was perhaps twelve years old. The call of Moses came during an ordinary work day in the form of a burning bush. Isaiah's call came during worship. But God's call came to the young boy during the night as he was sleeping in the shrine.

When the Lord speaks to Samuel the first time, the boy assumes it is Eli calling for him. All he knows at this time he knows from Eli. He goes to the priest and says, "Here I am, for you called me." But Eli sends him back to bed. This happens a second time and still the boy does not recognize the Lord. Only on the third approach does Eli tell Samuel that it is the Lord, not his teacher, who is speaking to him. At that moment Eli's role as teacher begins to decline, and the boy begins his rise as the leader of God's people.

Eli, being a good instructor, told the boy what to say when the call came again. Samuel followed the instructions, and when the call came he knew exactly what to say. Moses, you remember, was reluctant to hear all that God had in mind for him, but Samuel had youthful enthusiasm for the call, even though his task would be difficult and painful.

Samuel, the new prophet of the Lord, served God by speaking truth to the people, including Eli whose household was evil. Eli's sons were "worthless." We're told that Eli knew of the sins of his sons and had not disciplined them. Samuel's first task as prophet is to relay to Eli these words of judgment. He waits until morning and fears telling Eli of his vision. But when the old priest asks Samuel about his dream, he tells him everything.

Eli, preeminent in the life of this special child, raised Samuel for God and then stepped aside to let God "have" the young man. And before Eli, Hannah forfeited her control over her child and gave him to God. This is God's important call to the adults in our congregations and communities. God calls parents, grandparents, aunts, uncles, elders, and teachers to practice raising all children for God.

We are given a lot of information about the birth and childhood of Moses. We know that he was spared death by an ingenious mother. But in the case of Samuel, we learn that his mother dedicated him to God's service even before he was conceived.

Many Protestant denominations conduct a service of consecration for parents and children during the worship hour. The service provides opportunity for parents to consecrate their children to God. It is a time for parents to declare their intentions to instruct their children in the Christian way of life, even before they know the strengths and weaknesses of the children. Thus, as the children grow older, they will likely embrace Christianity as their faith.

Not only is the service of consecration a time for parents and children, but it includes a charge to the congregation. All the members of a congregation share responsibility for the faith formation and Christian nurture of its children. During the consecration the minister takes the child and lays hands on his or her head, declaring words such as, "This day you are dedicated to God, that all efforts of home, family, and church may bring you to the moment of your own decision for Jesus Christ."

The call came to Samuel because he was in the right place with the right person. He was set apart as a child to do God's work. Though we see no sudden, great transformation that changed Samuel into a spiritual leader, we're constantly reminded that Samuel grew "both in stature and in favor with the Lord and with the people." Like Jesus, who was in the temple when he was twelve, Samuel had a family that made sure he was surrounded by the influence of God's people.

The book *For All the Saints*, edited by Melanie May, includes a chapter by Lauree Hersch Meyer on calling and formation. Free-church traditions, she says, are most familiar with the notion of transformation, that spectacular experience of conversion. Transformation is, indeed, often dramatic. A person is recreated into someone quite different from who she once was. Transformation means radical change.

Meyer reminds us, however, that formation is quite different from transformation, and yet equally as important. Formation isn't as radical in nature as transformation. It happens over a long period of time. It is the way in which something gradually takes shape. Christian education has the task of shaping the lives of individuals in much the same way. Samuel was formed during the day-by-day process of life—first through the relationship with his parents and then through daily interactions with Eli in the temple.

At a service of consecration for parents and children, the parents and the congregation confront this challenge: Will they view the formation of each child's Christian identity as their own calling? For as children interact with the church members, these young people learn what the church really is. Meyer writes, "Given the church's vast and inescapable power to form the next generation, each church is called to nurture the next generation so that persons' formative experiences elicit trust and loyalty to God, love for the church, and passion to serve God in the world."

The call of Samuel while still a young boy reminds us of the church's task to provide our children and young people nurturing opportunities for growth. What are we doing to foster commitment to Christ and the church? In what ways are we preparing to lead our youth to accept God's call when it is extended?

Some congregations have set up a mentoring program whereby adult

members match up with young people in the congregation. It is not necessarily a highly structured program. But through it, mentors initiate periodic
contacts and build relationships with their young "disciples." The young
people know their mentors are particularly concerned with their welfare.
They realize they are upheld in prayer and are encouraged in spiritual mat-
ters. Certainly, the mentor is someone who can help with the question, How
is God calling me?

Discussion and Action

1. Share about any "call experiences" from your childhood or youth.
   Who helped you recognize or better understand the will of God for
   you at crucial decision points?
2. Name instances in which you, like young Samuel, have had diffi-
   culty determining whether you were hearing the voice of God?
3. What is the relationship between maturity and God's calling? How
   does God call young people today? What is the role of the church in
   helping any person understand a call?
4. Have you known a time when "the word of the Lord was rare," as
   in young Samuel's day? or a time when there was "frequent vision"?
5. What did it mean for Hannah to dedicate her son to God's service?
   How would you have felt after leaving Samuel with Eli? What things
   can parents do today as ways of dedicating their children to God?
6. All congregations need to foster an environment conducive to identifying and affirming gifts in their young people. How would you
   rate your own church in this regard? What creative ideas for im-
   provement might you suggest?

4

God Calls Ruth
Ruth 1–4

Ruth lived a holy life of service to God, doing naturally what God asks all of us to do. We cultivate the same natural response by practicing Christlike disciplines, including the greeting of one another as brothers and sisters in Christ.

Personal Preparation

1. Read the entire Book of Ruth. Read it for enjoyment, like any good story.
2. What does Ruth's story tell you about God's call in her life? in your life today?
3. Look back over your life for a few moments. Is there anything that you now understand as a call from God that was not recognized as a call at the time? How did you respond?

Understanding

During an otherwise dismal time in the life of the Hebrews, the story of Ruth emerges as the charming encounter of several kind people. In the end, two of them marry, and their union produces a son, Obed, grandfather of the great King David. A young foreign widow and a wealthy Jewish landowner thus bring new blood to the chosen race.

This story of Ruth is gentle, a tale without villains or violence. In the guise of a love story, the Book of Ruth challenges the old prejudice against "strangers." It widens God's covenant with the people to include faithful foreigners such as Ruth from Moab, an enemy land east of Judah. The account begins with the words, "In the days when the judges ruled . . . ," much like our "Once upon a time . . . ." We know a story is beginning.

The days of the judges percolated with bloodshed and warfare, with gruesome scenes recorded again and again in the Book of Judges. But Ruth's story, set in the same time period, is charming and gentle. Even though it begins with the report of a famine and the deaths of three men, it moves on to celebrate human kindness.

First we are introduced to four people: Elimelech, a man from Bethlehem; his wife, Naomi; and their two sons. We learn that a famine wracked their land, forcing them east, past the Dead Sea, in search of food. They remain in that place, the land of Moab, for ten years, with both sons marrying Moabite women.

But then Elimelech and his two sons die, leaving Naomi without a husband or a son—a terrible fate for a woman in ancient times. Not only does she lose her loved ones, she loses all financial support. She faces certain poverty and homelessness.

Finally, upon hearing that the famine is over in Bethlehem, Naomi and her daughters-in-law, Ruth and Orpah, begin the journey back. They hope to find security with Elimelech's family, who is obligated to help the dead relative's wife. Yet scarcely into the journey, Naomi concludes that it's not fair to take these women away from their home country. She decides to do the kind thing and send both of them back to their mothers. She hopes they will marry again and get on with their lives.

The women refuse to leave Naomi to journey on alone, but she is kindly insistent. She emphasizes that the life of a widow is hard and that their best hope is to return home, marry Moabite men, and start their own families. Naomi's kind offer makes sense to Orpah who, with tears, embraces, and kisses, returns to Moab. But Ruth will not turn back.

Upon reaching Bethlehem, the women receive an overwhelming reception. Naomi fears being rejected for having lived among the enemy and allowing her sons to intermarry. But her old friends come out to meet her and to meet for the first time Naomi's devoted daughter-in-law, Ruth, the Moabitess.

The story of kindness continues. Ruth immediately begins the chore of gathering food for herself and Naomi. An ancient practice encouraged farmers to allow the poor and hungry to glean anything left or spilled in the fields after the harvest. Thus, Ruth gathers grain in the field of Boaz, known as a good, kind, God-fearing man. He has already heard of Ruth because people have been talking of this young foreign widow who is loyal and kind to her mother-in-law.

Boaz authorizes his servants to leave large piles of grain in Ruth's path as she gleans. In this way, he becomes her supplier and her protector. And knowing that danger lurks in the fields for a foreign woman working alone, he puts out the word that anyone who harms Ruth will be at his mercy.

Naomi was kind to Ruth and Orpah. Orpah and Ruth were kind to Naomi.

Boaz was kind to Ruth and Naomi. What a story! How different from the stories of war, revenge, and hatred in the period of the Judges!

The story of Ruth settles into an unusual niche in this study of call and response. Unlike others who heard the voice of God quite clearly, Ruth received no formal and identifiable call. Though we clearly see that she enjoyed the blessing of God, we do better with hindsight in identifying Ruth as one called and chosen. Maybe that is precisely why more of us can identify with Ruth than with other biblical heroes. Sometimes it is only in looking back on our lives that we can ascertain a divine call. At the time we felt we were simply doing what we had to do, not what we were called to do by God.

We get the feeling that Ruth wasn't necessarily responding to a clear voice as she made certain choices along the way. Rather, it seems she was simply "just that kind of person." She had deep feelings of loyalty toward Naomi. When prudence said Ruth should leave her mother-in-law, she just couldn't.

The beautiful words in Ruth 1:16-17, oddly enough, are not the vows between a man and a woman in marriage; instead they are words spoken by a daughter-in-law to a bereaved, widowed, childless mother-in-law:

> Do not press me to leave you
>   or to turn back from following you!
> Where you go, I will go;
>   Where you lodge, I will lodge;
> your people shall be my people,
>   and your God my God.

The congregation I served for nearly twelve years was quite small, but we had six Ruths. We used to laugh and say that without them we would be a ruthless congregation! When I think back over the lives of these Ruths and other women in the congregation, I sincerely doubt if many of them would state with confidence that they had heard a call from God and responded yes. Rather, I think most would review their lives and say that through good and bad times they sensed God's presence in their lives. If pressed, a few might name certain experiences that could be identified as a call from God.

I think too often in the church we have unwittingly given a false impression that only ministers and other church professional types receive calls from God. The result is that if one isn't so inclined, he or she doesn't even think along the lines of a personal call.

When the topic of call is raised, it points to the reason why a person does what he or she does. But there is nothing in the Book of Ruth about motives. We simply encounter a story. We don't know why Ruth does what she does, but we do watch her make her choices. Paul's words in Romans 8:28 seem to fit here:

"We know that all things work together for good for those who love God, who are called according to his purpose." We need no other motive than that we love God and are persuaded that we must live Christlike lives.

The call to live a Christlike life is a call to live a disciplined life. We train our children how to live so they won't ask "why" each time they are asked to respond. They begin taking on responsibility automatically and naturally out of their training. As adults, we also practice Christian discipline by regular attendance at worship and regular support with our money, time, and talents. And we don't have to examine ourselves each time a call comes to us. We don't have to search for the impulse to be kind or wait on self-control when we are angry. As Christians we come by these responses naturally.

In our worship we also practice these disciplines. Take, for example, the holy kiss and passing the peace—"Greet one another with a kiss of love. Peace to all of you who are in Christ" (1 Pet. 5:14). The regular practice of greeting one another as children of God, whether we actually want to or not on a particular day, trains our impulses to be like God's. The call to love and respect others is more genuine when it is an unconscious act, a true impulse.

Like Ruth, we are not always conscious of God's claim upon our lives, but it is a strong claim. The impulse, the unconscious reaction of love, is a sign that God is at work in our lives.

Discussion and Action

1. Share about some of the times you can now identify as instances when you unwittingly responded to a call from God.
2. Why are the words spoken by a daughter-in-law to her mother-in-law (in Ruth 1:16-17) appropriate for use in a wedding? On what other occasions might they be fitting today?
3. What role do we play in helping others identify God's call in their lives?
4. How are the practices of the holy kiss, embracing, and passing the peace helpful symbols for congregational life today?
5. How has your church contributed to the idea that God's call is reserved exclusively for religious professionals? How do you (or could you) call others?
6. Who are some of the "Ruth-types" in your life, or in your congregation, who naturally make life good and full for others?

5

God Calls David
1 Samuel 16

David was the unexpected one, the youngest, and yet God told Samuel to anoint him as Israel's king. Through rituals such as the service of anointing, Christians identify those who are set apart and spirit-filled for Christian service.

Personal Preparation

1. Read 1 Samuel 16. What do you think it means to "look on the heart" when calling someone to leadership in the church?
2. When were you unexpectedly called out for a particular task? Or when have you helped to call someone who may have been an unexpected choice?
3. Have you ever been anointed as part of a call to leadership? If so, what did this mean to you?

Understanding

If you've ever had the opportunity to serve on a pastoral search committee, you know how difficult that process can be. Early on, the committee must face its own unreasonable expectations, realizing that it wants a man with years and years of experience yet young enough to relate well with the youth. Often the church wants a seminary-trained person willing to work on the pay scale of a high school graduate. And soon the committee must address hard questions about the congregation's willingness to call a woman, or a person from a different culture, or someone with no prior experience. Serving on a search committee is a tough assignment.

Samuel, in this passage, is functioning as a one-man search committee. Although the Lord made Saul the anointed king over Israel, the task falls to Samuel to tell Saul that the Lord is rejecting him. Not only does Samuel need to search for a new leader, he has to tell the old king that he is fired! The task is almost too much for Samuel.

First, according to God's instruction, Samuel is to take his anointing oil and go to the house of Jesse in Bethlehem to choose a new king from among Jesse's several sons. But to get to Bethlehem, Samuel has to pass through Gibeah, the home of Saul. He is understandably afraid that his mission to anoint the future king will anger Saul. God suggests that Samuel proceed as if his real mission is a sacrifice to the Lord. Jesse and his sons will be invited to attend the sacrifice, and there Samuel can review the candidates and name a new king.

When Samuel sees the sons, he is immediately impressed by the first-born, Eliab. But God says to Samuel, "Do not look on his appearance or on the height of his stature, because I have rejected him; for the Lord does not see as mortals see; they look on the outward appearance, but the Lord looks on the heart" (16:7). Samuel has to take care that he does not judge the future king by society's standards, but rather, he looks on the heart as God does. After all, the people chose Saul and their choice failed. The choice is not Samuel's anyway. The choice for the new king is God's. In fact, Samuel tells Saul that "the Lord has torn the kingdom of Israel from you this very day, and has given it to a neighbor of yours, who is better than you" (15:28).

Eventually, seven sons of Jesse pass before Samuel, but none are God's apparent choice. "Are all your sons here?" Samuel asks Jesse. Only David remains, the youngest, a shepherd. They send for him and when he arrives, God says to Samuel, "Rise and anoint him; for this is the one" (16:12).

With his oil Samuel anoints David in the presence of all his brothers. We're told that "the spirit of the Lord came mightily upon David from that day forward." Verse 18 describes David as "a man of valor, a warrior, prudent in speech, and a man of good presence; and the Lord is with him."

In the accounts of 1 Samuel, the task of anointing falls to Samuel. Not only does he anoint David, he is the one who anointed Saul king of Israel. In the Old Testament, anointing was a symbol of the presence and activity of the Holy Spirit. While it was reserved mainly for kings (the Lord's anointed), we sometimes read of the anointing of priests (Exod. 29:7) and the anointing of prophets (1 Kgs. 19:16). Based on James 5 in the New Testament, some denominations practice anointing for healing, physically and spiritually. In every case, anointing calls for the presence of God.

Brethren pastor Guy E. Wampler, writes: "The church needs poignant symbols . . . particularly for services of installation and for healing. . . . the symbol [of anointing] lifts before us timely dimensions of our faith. In the present world, in which some are prone to feel small, almost defeated, isolated, ill, or uncommitted, the theme of 'anointed!' fosters the spirit of gladness, royalty, hospitality, healing, and consecration. Anointed! It is God's call and God's grace made personal."

As often as we eat of the bread and drink of the cup, we proclaim God's call upon our lives. When we remember our baptism, we are reminded of God's call upon our lives. And through the ritual of anointing, we can symbolize our call as set apart for God's purpose. These acts all serve to remind us of who we are: The ones called by God.

The church is to identify those unexpected ones who might be good candidates for set-apart ministries. Like Samuel, we are often initially attracted to more obvious candidates. When we think of good ministers, we often think of men, men who are mature, married, middle-aged, musical, and modest. If indeed these are the only criteria for a good leader, perhaps there is great truth in the rumor of a leadership crisis in the church.

In *For All the Saints*, Lauree Hersch Meyer writes:

> We hear of a leadership crisis in the church, but we are not clear what this means. Whose leadership crisis is it? Not all of us experience a leadership crisis. . . . There is a vast pool of persons who have not traditionally been in leadership who are eager to be called into set-apart ministry—women, people of color, and ethnic people—even though the pool of traditional faces, white and male, is smaller. We are not sure if Anglo church members are willing to accept "others" as leaders. Inasmuch as we do not accept "others," we create the leadership crisis. (19)

I have always taken the church seriously. Even as a child, I played church, lining up the dining room chairs and preaching to a congregation of dolls and teddy bears. We went as a family to church on Sunday morning and Sunday and Wednesday evenings. When I grew older, my church encouraged me to attend the Bible college they supported. Happily, I felt called to begin my training for whatever form of Christian service God would have for me.

On the Sunday I was to travel five hundred miles to enroll in a college I had never seen, the preacher wished me Godspeed from the pulpit. I'll never forget his comments. In front of everyone, he said his hope was that I would meet and marry a good preacher boy and serve God all my days as a pastor's wife. A high calling to be sure, but his notion of what was possible for a college-bound Christian girl was too fixed and narrow.

Samuel's call and anointing of David ought to raise important questions for us. For example, how do our congregations identify and call young people from our midst? When we see a bright, gifted, young person, do we see gifts for ministry within that person? Do we see them as potential doctors, lawyers, or corporate executives? On career days at school, what professions do we encourage our own children to investigate and consider? As we drive home from worship on Sunday, what impressions do we leave with our children as to our feelings about pastoral leadership?

Have you ever encouraged someone to consider the possibility of full-time Christian service? How many people from your church have been licensed, ordained, or gone to seminary in the last ten years? These questions all get to the heart of how involved your congregation is in the calling process.

Does your denomination and/or congregation practice anointing for leadership? If so, what is involved in the ritual? In my own church, these are some of the words spoken as a person is anointed with oil:

> _____, upon your confession of faith in the love and power of God, your willingness to commit your life completely to God in sickness or in health, and your desire to live your life for God's glory, you are now being anointed with oil in the name of the Lord . . . .

Though the anointing service is still most often carried out on behalf of a sick person, we might do well to consider, What better "confession" of dedication could we ask from our potential spiritual leaders?

Discussion and Action

1. In practical terms, what does it mean to you to "look on the heart" rather than on outward appearance? When in daily life do you apply this principle? How can we see into someone's heart?

2. Talk about times when you were unexpectedly called out for a particular task. How did you feel? How did you respond?

3. In your opinion, is there a leadership crisis or a faith crisis in the church today? Are we overlooking potential leaders because they don't fit the mold? If possible, offer some examples.

4. Would your congregation be open to calling a woman or a person of a different ethnic background to serve as its pastor? How would you personally respond to this?

5. If David ran for president of the United States, would you vote for him? Could he be elected?

6. How can anointing be appropriate for both healing and for consecration of those called to serve? Do the two meanings of the symbol have anything in common?

7. To symbolize the call to leadership and service in Christ's church and a willing response, consider anointing the forehead or hands of all members of your group.

6

God Calls Jeremiah
Jeremiah 1:1-19

*God called Jeremiah to a formidable task: to be a prophet with
an unpopular message among people who did not want to listen. Today, the service of ordination recognizes that the church
has taken seriously the training and equipping of prophetic
leaders. This is crucial, for the task of spiritual leadership is
still difficult.*

Personal Preparation

1. Reflect upon any occasion when you were called to a particularly
   difficult task. Did you sense that God was with you as you responded
   to the call?
2. Read Jeremiah 1:1-19. How might you have responded to such a call?
3. What are some of the difficult calls that come to prophets today? to
   those called out and ordained for ministry?

Understanding

Jeremiah received God's call as a young man. He was called to be a prophet
to the nations, an enormous task. He was commanded to speak unpopular
truths, to confront the sins of the people. But key to this account is God's
promise that Jeremiah would be equipped for the work ahead. We're told
that God had Jeremiah in mind for the job even before he was born.

Dr. Martin Luther King, Jr., was a Jeremiah for his time. He was called
by the Dexter Avenue Baptist Church in Montgomery, Alabama, to be their
pastor just as racial tensions were reaching a boiling point in the South. He
was fresh out of graduate school at Boston University, and before that he attended Morehouse College and Crozer Seminary. King struggled with the
decision of whether to become a professor or a preacher. But when the call

was extended, he accepted a call to the ministry, following in the footsteps of his father, grandfather, and great-grandfather. He preached his first sermon in May of 1954.

That same month the US Supreme Court handed down its Brown vs. Board of Education decision, which outlawed segregation in public schools. Then in December 1955 Rosa Parks, after an exhausting day at work, boarded a city bus and sat near the front, the section reserved for whites. When a white man got on, Rosa refused to give her seat to him. She was tired and her feet hurt. Police arrested her and took her to the police station, where she was charged with violating the city segregation code. The city was Montgomery, Alabama, the new home of Martin Luther King, Jr.

The black church leaders of Montgomery came together to organize a nonviolent boycott of the bus line. But first the clergy group needed to elect officers. King was chosen as president. He had twenty minutes to prepare a speech for the thousands that had gathered. In *Let the Trumpet Sound*, King's biographer, Stephen B. Oates, writes, "It had all come pouring out in sixteen minutes of inspired extemporizing. It was as though he had been preparing for this speech all his life—as though his doubts and reaffirmations about the ministry, his courses and readings and reflections in college, had been intended for this ringing moment. . . . For the first time he understood what older preachers meant when they said, 'Open your mouth and God will speak for you.'"

Jeremiah described his own experience similarly. "Then the Lord put out his hand and touched my mouth; and the Lord said to me, 'Now I have put my words in your mouth'" (1:9). Both prophets, Jeremiah and Martin Luther King, Jr., were called to enormous tasks. And both were equipped, not as much with natural talent as by the gifts endowed to them by God. God gave them their words.

We find the ordination of Jeremiah in verse 9, where the Lord touches the young man's mouth. With this act he is commissioned to the task of declaring the word of the Lord. The prophet's task is twofold. Certain things must be done and other things undone. In the job description (v. 10), God commands four ways to undo the sins of the people: "to pluck up and to break down, to destroy and to overthrow." God tells Jeremiah that what is to be done to restore the people to faith is "to build and to plant." Words of salvation often meet with applause, but words of judgment usually inspire anger. Even Jeremiah himself didn't like his message. He often wept as he spoke, earning the title "The Weeping Prophet."

Ordination, such as Jeremiah's or King's, is the commissioning of a person for service to God's kingdom. God lays hands on the right person at the right time and God's people, the body of Christ, call to that person. There is no touching of the candidate's lips in our services of ordination, as in Jeremiah's, but there is the laying on of hands with a prayer that the Holy Spirit equip and empower the one called.

The church must take seriously its call to equip its members for the tasks of ministry. It is not fair to call and not train. Even God did not call out Jeremiah and then leave him unequipped. In 2 Timothy 2:15 (KJV), an elder in the faith encourages a young man to "study to show thyself approved unto God, a workman that needeth not to be ashamed, rightly dividing the word of truth." In Ephesians 4:12, we read that the church should "equip the saints for the work of ministry." Every congregation can make sure that its people, especially its young, have opportunities for Christian nurture and spiritual growth.

A century ago the new Sunday school movement was very controversial in some denominations. Some people feared that the church was robbing parents of their responsibility to give their own children religious education. One denomination, the Church of the Brethren, decided in 1838 that it was "most advisable to take part in no such things." Yet later, Sunday schools flourished and the church affirmed Christian education both at home and in the church. We know now that early training in congregational life and worship is important training for leaders.

The call to ordained ministry can be a monumental assignment, and solid support from the congregation provides a foundation upon which to build seminary experience. But training must begin early. In Jeremiah's case, consecration came even before he was born. Child development specialists tell us that our formation does indeed begin in the womb and that a child learns half of everything he or she will ever know by the age of three. How critical, then, is the early foundational training our future leaders receive in their congregations!

His call from God was clear, but Jeremiah feared that he was not up to the task. God assured him, though, that "I am with you." God made it clear that Jeremiah's enemies would fight against him, but God also promised that they would not be victorious. Nevertheless, a great challenge lay ahead. "Gird up your loins. . . . Do not break down before them. . . . They will fight against you; but they shall not prevail against you, for I am with you, says the Lord, to deliver you" (vv. 17-19).

People called to Christian service today also have enemies, and we must train our ministers to face their adversaries courageously and wisely. The thirteenth time Martin Luther King, Jr., was arrested and jailed, eight white Christian and Jewish clergy of Alabama signed a statement saying that King's work was untimely and unwise. Thus, even his own colleagues rejected him. In response to the statement, King wrote a rebuttal from his cell.

In part it reads:

> When I was suddenly catapulted into the leadership of the bus protest in Montgomery, Alabama, a few years ago, I felt we would be supported by the white church. I felt that the white ministers, priests and rabbis of the South would be among our strongest allies. Instead, some have been outright opponents, refusing to understand the freedom movement and misrepresenting its leaders; all too many others have been more cautious than courageous and have remained silent behind the anesthetizing security of stained-glass windows.

King wrote his letter with a pen smuggled into his cell by his lawyers. He began composing it along the margins of a newspaper and finished it on toilet paper. He had no research books or notes to work from in his dreary cell. But he was a workman schooled and trained by the church for the task, supremely difficult, to which God had called him.

Discussion and Action

1. Share stories of call to a difficult task, especially in the life of the church.
2. If God does the calling, why do we still need to prepare ourselves for ministry? What role does studying play in calling?
3. Have you heard a speaker whose lips seemed to have been touched by God? Has God ever touched your lips?
4. What role does the church play in the formation of future prophets? Have you ever known a church to call a person for a particular task and then not equip him or her to carry out the work well?
5. When is the church called to pluck up and to pull down, to destroy and to overthrow? If possible, suggest some practical examples.
6. Was Martin Luther King, Jr., ready for leadership because God had singled him out and prepared him? Or was he called because he was ready?
7. Think of people in your congregation whom you think God may be calling to ordained ministry. Decide whether to talk with your pastor, church board members, or ministry commission about issuing a call.

7

God Calls Isaiah
Isaiah 6

Isaiah is called by God while worshiping in the temple. How can we structure our worship so that people hear the call of God?

Personal Preparation

1. Read the scripture prayerfully at least once each day during the week.
2. Look at some recent bulletins or orders of worship. Choose several to take to the covenant group.
3. Look at the hymn "Let All Mortal Flesh Keep Silence" (p. 58). Read or sing it to yourself during the week.

Understanding

William Willimon begins his book *Worship as Pastoral Care* with this paragraph:

> Pity the poor pastor. The pastor has borne the brunt of an avalanche of criticism in recent years, has been told that he or she preaches poorly to a conglomeration of mostly comfortable and increasingly empty pews, that the church is a doomed and decaying institution, that what he or she does is of little lasting consequence anyway . . . all this amidst long hours, poor pay, and demanding parishioners. Just before the pastor collapses into bed at night, exhausted from the daily routine of visitation, training, teaching, sermon preparation, recruiting new members, church financial woes, and refereeing in congregational squabbles . . . she must muster up deep concern for yet one more area of church life—worship.

The first time I read this paragraph I was a pastor and responsible for planning the worship services for my congregation. Some weeks the time I spent planning for worship seemed like just one more thing added onto a very busy schedule. But I grew to enjoy those times of planning and set aside time each week to prepare for Sunday morning. Worship is central to the life of a Christian community. You can have a church and not have potlucks or carry-in dinners (heaven forbid!). You can have a church and not have a Sunday school. You can have a church and not have a mission society or daycare facilities. You can even have a church and not have a pastor. But you cannot have a church without worship.

The first worship services I planned were organized on the principle that everything must be coordinated. If the sermon, the kernel of the service, was to be about forgiveness, so would the scripture, the hymns, the prayers, and the children's story.

Worship would be coordinated all right, but many times my preoccupation with themes made worship much too narrow to meet the needs of all the people. Wise teachers helped me find a better way of planning and leading worship.

Isaiah 6 is essentially an order of worship that helps me honor God in more ways than one. It begins with a time of praise. A time of confession is followed by an assurance of pardon. There is then a call extended with an opportunity for a response.

Structure in our worship functions like the skeleton for the human body. Since many interrelated parts need to find their proper place, the elements that make up a worship service cannot be haphazardly strewn together. The assembled congregation certainly benefits from knowing the order of worship and becoming familiar with its structure.

Some people may argue that the leading of the Holy Spirit, not "structure," guides our worship. But a familiar pattern allows for flexibility and variation. My husband was always strict about a fixed bedtime for our daughters. They seemed to know that when that certain hour approached it was time to start heading for bed. Of course, exceptions arose, but they were not handled casually. That may sound rigid, but it made for two well-rested, happy children each morning. Structure actually gives more than it takes away.

It was in the context of a structured worship, with a regular time set aside for calling, that Isaiah received and accepted God's instruction. Thus, a central question for this session is: "Does our worship include rituals that call people to a life of service for God?"

Isaiah's description of his calling would challenge any Hollywood special-effects director. God sits high upon the throne, flowing robes filling the whole temple. Imagine! Six-winged, flying creatures calling out "Holy,

Holy, Holy!" Temple foundations shaking and the whole place filling with smoke! There is something to smell, feel, hear, and see.

Isaiah is completely humbled. His first reaction to this theophany (a vision of God) is to recognize his own sinfulness. In the presence of God's holiness, Isaiah senses his own unholiness. But renewal comes as one of the creatures takes a burning coal from the altar, touches Isaiah's lips, and declares, "Your sin is blotted out!"

Notice the structure of this service of worship. It begins with a time of praise as Isaiah encounters the presence of God. Just as the seraphim sang "Holy, Holy, Holy" at the beginning of this service, we too can sing hymns of praise as we gather to worship. Beginning with a time of praise helps us to recall and proclaim the real purpose of life. The old Westminster catechism asks the question, "What is the chief end of man?" The response is "to glorify God and to enjoy him forever."

From a time of praise, the service moves into a time of confessing our sins. When we come into God's presence, like Isaiah, we face our unholiness. Just as we must teach our children to say "thank you," we must also teach them to say "I'm sorry." This time of penitence flows from the time of praise. The God who loves us wants us to be in right relationship. This kind of affirmation and acceptance first allowed Isaiah to be overwhelmed with his uncleanness and then eager to serve as God's messenger just moments later. He did not have to wallow in his unworthiness. He was forgiven and could go on. The words of grace, "Your sin is forgiven," were spoken and believed.

Isaiah then overheard a call coming from God, "Whom shall I send?" With no hesitation Isaiah volunteered, "Here am I; send me." Similarly, the call to follow Jesus often comes to us through the reading of the scriptures and the preaching of the sermon. For us to have the openness to the call that Isaiah had, we need to examine our attitudes about the worship experience. Sunday morning is not a time for passive spectators. In order to hear God call our names, we must be attentive and receptive.

When a person hears God call, he or she needs an opportunity to respond to that call. Thus, worship concludes with a time of dedicating ourselves and our gifts to God, an act that can take many creative forms. We usually think of placing our money in the offering plate, but the time of dedication includes offering our whole lives, our time, and our talents to the service of Christ.

In some denominations, each worship service includes the Lord's Supper. An invitation to the table is extended, and the participants in worship move to accept the gifts of God. Some churches issue an altar call at the conclusion of the service, inviting those who have made decisions of faith to proclaim them publicly. Each service, depending on its theme, can offer a unique means of response. For example, after a sermon on "coming home" (related to the Prodigal

Son parable), one pastor invited everyone into the church basement for a piece of apple pie—and sharing about the joys and sorrows of family life.

A college student studying Spanish made it a practice for several years to sit with Spanish-speaking people during the worship services at her national church conferences. She liked to sit in the reserved section and practice the language by listening to the translation of the service. One day, after having worshiped in Spanish many times, she was suddenly struck by a profound sensation that God wanted her to do something with her gift for language. She felt a calling and soon afterward responded by volunteering with a church agency, taking on a life of voluntary poverty and ministering to people in Latin America.

During worship, the call of God can ring out loud and clear. So as you settle into your pew next Sunday, ask yourself: What kind of voice do I expect to hear?

Discussion and Action

1. Do you function mostly as a participant or as a spectator in worship? To what extent are you open to hearing a call from God on an average Sunday morning?
2. Describe a worship service in which you felt filled with wonder, love, and praise.
3. Look at some of the worship bulletins from your church. Can you find in them all the elements of worship given in Isaiah 6?
4. Is your worship conducive to calling people into Christian service? Is there a logical place in the worship service for a person to respond to a call? Must the opportunity always be public in nature?
5. Isaiah went to the temple in the year King Uzziah died, when all stability was threatened. Yet at this time God called and Isaiah responded. Where do you go when your foundations have been shaken? Have you ever heard God's call at such a time?
6. When have you said, "Here am I, send me"?
7. Close by singing or reading together the words of the hymn "Let All Mortal Flesh Keep Silence" (p. 58).

8

God Calls Mary
Luke 1:39-56

Mary heard the call: "Give birth to the world's Savior!" She responded with, "Let it be." Today, the service of feetwashing is a reminder that we are to accept as well as serve.

Personal Preparation

1. Gather pictures of Mary, particularly of the Annunciation. Old Christmas cards and Christmas postage stamps often have great pictures. Take some of your favorites to the group.
2. Read Luke 1:39-56. Think: When have I received a call (from God or from another person) that gave me astounding and unexpected news?
3. How easy is it for you as an adult to say "let it be" and allow yourself to be held up by God?

Understanding

As I write, it is early November and the house down the street is already decorated with twinkling Christmas lights. I laugh at my neighbors who hurry the holiday season along and revel in the celebration for weeks. Possibly I'm glad to see lights on his house because I'm clearly not brazen enough to put them on mine just yet. But there is something about Christmas none of us can resist.

Madeleine L'Engle reflects on the church year in her book *The Irrational Season*. She claims that Christmas is *irrational*, not in the usual sense that people go overboard and spend money they don't have or light their houses two months in advance. Rather, the season is irrational in that it is based upon truths beyond our capacity to reason.

Think of what the announcement of Jesus' coming meant to Mary. Nothing in Gabriel's message made any sense to her. For years I have been fascinated by the great variety of paintings on the theme of the Annunciation, the encounter between Mary and the angel Gabriel. My favorite is by Fr. Angelica. In this masterpiece, the bewinged Gabriel has evidently just told Mary the news because her look is a questioning "Me?" Simone Martini's *Annunciation* amuses me. In his painting, Gabriel has clearly disturbed Mary's reading and she looks to be in a very sour mood. Most renderings of the event seem to hint that none of it makes sense.

The details of the Annunciation come through in Luke 1:26-27. In the sixth month of Elizabeth's pregnancy, the angel Gabriel comes from God to give Mary a message. Mary is a virgin, betrothed to a man named Joseph. Gabriel's greeting is nice enough, but meetings with angels are rare and mystifying for Mary. The Gospels later describe her as one who ponders things in her heart. That characteristic is evident here, as well, as she tries to sort out exactly what the angel means by "Greetings, favored one! The Lord is with you!"

Nothing in the story is ordinary. Perhaps the most amazing thing is that Mary does not seem to be afraid. If possible, search a biblical concordance for all the references to "Do not be afraid" or "Fear not." Throughout the biblical story God speaks these words of assurance. They are particularly comforting when one's name is attached, as when the angel says, "Do not be afraid, Mary."

Mary receives the word that God had taken special notice of her and has chosen her to bear a son. She is even given the child's name. Logic tells us that a child whose birth announcement springs from an angel's lips will not be an ordinary child! Gabriel describes the child who will be called Jesus as the one who will reign on the throne of David, not just for his lifetime but forever.

Mary sorts through the message and knows that to have a child she needs to be married to Joseph, which she isn't—yet. So in response to her call, she, like Moses and Jeremiah and others before, questions the messenger. She asks, "How can this be, since I am a virgin?"

Essentially, Gabriel says it is possible, "For nothing is impossible with God." Mary is reminded that Elizabeth, once considered barren, is now six months pregnant, joining the long line of biblical woman who were once barren. The motherhood of Sarah, Hannah, Rachel, and Rebecca had once been doubtful . . . and then became real. So Mary accepts the call easily and bravely with the words: "Here am I, the servant of the Lord; let it be with me according to your word." Once Gabriel had his answer he was gone.

Mary is now pregnant and has a lot of explaining to do. Granted, being chosen out of all women anywhere and anytime is an incredible honor. Generations of people would call her blessed. But she still has to break the news to Joseph, give birth, and then raise the one who would change the world forever.

Look at the common thread that runs through the verses of Luke 1:29; 2:19; and 2:51. While Mary accepted the call readily, she also seemed always to be processing something in her mind and heart. She was, in the language of spirituality, "discerning." More often than not, when a call comes, we too ask God for guidance and clarity. We're not being irreverent; we are puzzling over a call that may be ambiguous and confusing.

In his book on discernment, *Weeds Among the Wheat*, Jesuit Thomas Green writes, "A discerning person must always be humble, charitable and courageous." These words could describe Mary. She courageously risks accepting her call, even though she doesn't know all the answers. She is a discerning person whose trust in God has led her to accept first and ask questions later. Do we have that sort of trust in God?

I'm petrified of deep water. I've taken swimming lessons many times as a child and as an adult, and I always pass the beginner's portion with flying colors. I can float on my back and hold my head under water. I can even swim the width of the pool. But when the time comes to go to the deep end, I drop the course. In my mind I cannot perceive the water as a friend capable of holding me up. To me it's an enemy about to destroy me, and I fight back. My goal is to learn to trust the water, to let it be.

Whether I fight the water or surrender to it, the result will be the same. I need to keep in mind the sensation I have when I float in three feet of water. Thomas Green calls it "dynamic receptivity." If we let go, God will support us.

That, I think, is the conclusion of Mary's pondering. She could have fought the divine call. She could have even turned away and ignored the messenger. Or she could exercise dynamic receptivity and be an active participant in God's plan to bring Jesus into the world.

Oddly, it is not in the Christmas season, with all its irrationality, that we experience this kind of trust and acceptance. It is in the reenactment of the Lord's Supper, and particularly in the service of feetwashing as practiced by some denominations, that we know true acceptance of God's call for us.

We usually think of feetwashing as a service we do *for* someone. It is symbolic of Christian service and sacrifice. But according to the account in John 13, the disciples first *received* the loving action of feetwashing before performing it for others. Peter objected at first, refusing to let the Lord wash his feet. But Jesus insisted, saying, "Unless I wash you, you have no share with me" (13:8).

Unless we accept and trust Jesus, we cannot know the endless grace of God. Unless we learn to accept first and ask questions later, we will never enter into the difficult tasks God has in mind for us. By this world's standards, God's expectations are completely irrational. And yet, in the end, they are the only thing that will keep us afloat.

So "let it be."

Discussion and Action

1. Share your pictures of Mary. What feelings do these pictures arouse in you? Is Mary a role model in the faith for you?
2. Compare and contrast the call of Mary with the call of Ruth.
3. Mary carefully pondered her call. But Moses and Jeremiah questioned their calls. Does that make these two men less faithful than those who had no objections or questions? Explain.
4. Given Mary's nature of pondering things in her heart and mind, compare her to someone you know who has that same tendency. How is pondering different from worrying?
5. In what ways are you like Peter, who didn't want Jesus to wash his feet? To what extent would you say you trust God in daily situations? for your life's direction? Can you accept the call and ponder it later?
6. Conclude by singing (or saying together) the hymn, "When Peace, Like a River":

> When peace, like a river, attendeth my way,
> When sorrows like sea billows roll;
> Whatever my lot, Thou has taught me to say,
> "It is well, it is well with my soul."
> —Horatio G. Spafford

9

God Calls Paul and Ananias
Acts 9:1-19

Paul undergoes a radical transformation when he experiences the call of God. Ananias, whose call is less dramatic, performs the laying on of hands, and Paul regains his sight. What is the significance of laying on of hands today?

Personal Preparation

1. Read Acts 9:1-19. How would you retell the story of these two calls (and the two responses)—so that a first-grader could understand what happened?
2. Think of your own vocation. In what ways do you see your work as a Christian calling?
3. Reflect upon the practice of laying on of hands. Have you ever experienced this practice or observed or participated in it? What meanings and feelings does it hold for you?

Understanding

Seminarians today tend to be older than the typical seminarians of past decades. Many people are entering seminary after having established a career in a different field. It's not unusual for a church to hire a person new to the ministry but with years of experience in the business world. Second-career students add a new and refreshing dimension to the life of our seminaries and ministry in our churches.

These students often remark how their prior training and experience prove useful in their ministry. It seems that whatever we learn is never wasted. But I had to remind myself of this when our high school freshman moaned, "I'll never need this algebra when I get to Hollywood!" Most of us only see the value of our learning and experience in hindsight.

Paul was well trained. He had the best teachers. He studied at the feet of Gamaliel, a famous teacher who once persuaded an angry mob of Jews from killing a group of Christians. He reasoned with them, saying, "I tell you, keep away from these men and let them alone; because if this plan or this undertaking is of human origin, it will fail; but if it is of God, you will not be able to overthrow them . . . you may even be found fighting against God" (Acts 5:38-39). This short scene foreshadows Saul's encounter with the Lord when Saul hears, "I am Jesus, whom you are persecuting" (9:5). Only in hindsight does Paul appreciate the full meaning of Gamaliel's teaching!

Paul had an impressive pedigree. He wasn't just an ordinary Jew, he was a Pharisee. J. B. Phillips describes the Pharisees as the Puritans of their day. They demanded strict adherence to the law and purged the Jewish community of blasphemers and sinners. Paul was this zealous sort; in fact, when we're first introduced to him, he is a witness to the execution of Stephen. The crowd dragged Stephen out of the city to stone him and "the witnesses laid their coats at the feet of a young man named Saul" (Acts 7:58). Paul was not merely an onlooker, a bystander. In Jewish law the ones who witnessed an execution were considered to be among the executioners.

By his own admission, Paul was a ruthless persecutor. In Galatians Paul writes, "You have no doubt heard of my earlier life in Judaism. I was violently persecuting the church of God and was trying to destroy it. I advanced in Judaism beyond many among my people of the same age, for I was far more zealous for the traditions of my ancestors" (1:13).

At the time of his conversion, Paul is on his way to Damascus to search for followers of Jesus. He is authorized by the high priest of the temple to bring the offenders to Jerusalem as prisoners. We get the idea that Paul worked on a commission.

As Paul nears Damascus, he is struck by a blazing light so bright that it knocks him to the ground. With the light comes a voice: "Saul, Saul, why do you persecute me?" It is Jesus. If Jesus' followers are persecuted, Jesus himself is being persecuted.

This encounter causes Paul to lose his sight, a phenomenon he calls a "heavenly vision" (Acts 26:19) and an appearance (1 Cor. 15:8). However we describe the event, we know it left Paul a changed man. Heading toward Damascus with every intention of rounding up more followers of the Way (as early Christianity was called), he is instead led into the city, completely dependent upon his guide because he cannot see. In a moment Paul's vocation is changed, for God has a new calling for him.

But Paul isn't the only one seeing visions. A Christian in Damascus named Ananias is called by the Lord to inquire about Paul. Ananias has heard of Paul's reputation and questions the wisdom of showing concern for such an evil man, but the Lord convinces Ananias that Paul has been chosen to witness to Gentiles and Jews.

Ananias approaches Paul, lays his hands on him, and calls him "Brother." This took enormous faith and forgiveness. Ananias had been sent to lift the blindness, to be a conduit of the Holy Spirit. With the laying on of hands, Ananias delivered God's call to a new life. We're told Paul rose and was baptized, took food and was strengthened.

Both Paul and Ananias received calls, and their responses were uniquely their own. Paul responded, "Who are you, Lord?" Ananias said, "Here I am, Lord." These two men were clearly at different places in their lives. Ananias was a disciple charged with calling out Paul's gifts. Paul was converting his gift of energy from a destructive thing to a productive force that would glorify God.

Calls from God do not take the same form. As you've studied these lessons, you've seen that each call was unique. It was true during biblical times; it's true today as well. People are led into various kinds of vocations in a multitude of ways. Each person's experience is unique. That is why it is so fascinating to hear the stories.

My sister-in-law is a deeply committed Christian and a nurse. She is the home health care nurse within a hospice unit of our local hospital. She spends her days attending to dying people and their families in their homes. She is gentle and thoughtful, and people with whom she ministers love her. I've been with her in public settings and people make a special point to approach and greet her and tell her about their lives. After such an encounter she usually says something to us like, "I took care of their mother last year before she died. They were such a nice family." Her calling is one of a kind because it blends her unique talents with a particular need. Since everyone is different, every call will be one of a kind.

While studying this passage, we usually focus all of our attention on Paul, but as church people we must observe the role played by Ananias, too. A disciple already, he was used by God to be at the right place at the right time to receive the future apostle. It is clear that Jesus called Paul, but Ananias became the human instrument whereby hands were laid upon Paul so that he received the Holy Spirit and regained his sight. As church members, we have a role to play in receiving and nurturing those in our midst who are called by God.

Notice that when Ananias first approached Paul he functioned as an agent of God, laying his hands on Paul. This was an act of one in leadership, bestowing a gift upon one who would soon be in leadership himself. Even today, the laying on of hands symbolizes the Holy Spirit coming upon a person for the wisdom and authority to lead.

Every time we commission leaders or consecrate children or baptize new members, I can again feel the pressure of the hands laid upon me at my own ordination. Someone called out my gifts and changed my life. Now we must lay hands on each person in the church, converting their talents and energy to Christ's service.

Discussion and Action

1. Share your thinking about your own work or job as a calling or a vocation. What makes it "Christian work" for you?
2. Contrast the callings of Paul and Ananias. Which call would be closer to your own experience?
3. How useful do you think Paul's prior religious training was when he became a Christian missionary?
4. Recall the different times you have seen, experienced, or participated in the laying on of hands. What is the meaning of this ritual for you?
5. Why would people leave an established career and go to seminary to enter the ministry? Do you know any people who have done this? Talk about their motivations and sense of calling.
6. How does your congregation go about identifying gifts for leadership? How can you do this in your class or group?
7. Can you name people in your congregation whose gifts for leadership you can call out?

10

God Calls Disciples
Matthew 9:35—10:4

Jesus gave a new vocation to his disciples. But he also autho-rized and empowered them before sending them out. What does the church do to authorize those it commissions today?

Personal Preparation

1. Read Matthew 9:35—10:4. Think about why Jesus called a number of disciples.
2. In a brief paragraph, write what you think compassion means.
3. Recall different commissioning services you have attended or been a part of in your congregation. Read from your denominational book of worship to become familiar with its commissioning services.

Understanding

I have often been greatly humbled by the ability of others to be compassion-ate. There was a time some years ago when I had taken on several attractive assignments and then found myself overextended. For a few weeks, before I could see my way clear, I kept imagining myself dangling from a cliff by my fingernails. I was so preoccupied with my obligations that I had to feign in-terest in the people I was supposed to be helping in my work at the local refugee resettlement office. I'd answer the phone to hear a person with very limited English seeking help with a problem. But quite frankly I often didn't care.

I would watch the founding director of the program, who seemed to have an infinite capacity to respond compassionately to nearly everything that came her way. She faced enormous obstacles of funding and support for her important program, yet she kept on.

During that time, I thought a lot about the word *compassion*. Donald McNeil, Douglas Morrison, and Henri Nouwen wrote a book a few years ago called *Compassion: A Reflection on the Christian Life*. They say: "The word *compassion* is derived from the Latin words *pati* and *cam*, which together mean 'to suffer with.' Compassion asks us to go where it hurts, to enter into places of pain, to share in brokenness, fear, confusion and anguish. . . . Therefore compassion is not among our natural responses." Our natural impulse is to avoid these troubles.

In this scripture Jesus goes about teaching, preaching, and healing. "When he saw the crowds, he had compassion for them, because they were harassed and helpless, like sheep without a shepherd. Then . . . " (9:36). Then what?

What would be the response of the Compassionate One to this miserable crowd? As a result of the compassion he felt for the lost, Jesus called together twelve disciples and gave them authority to carry on the work he had started, that of teaching, preaching, and healing. Just as God heard the cries of Israel enslaved in Egypt and called Moses to lead the people into freedom, Jesus was moved by the pitiful crowd in the Galilean countryside and called his disciples to minister in his name.

A Presbyterian minister, Frederick Buechner, has written a provocative book entitled *Wishful Thinking*. Writing on vocation, Buechner refers to the Latin *vocare*, which means "to call." Buechner suggests:

> A good rule for testing the kind of work God usually calls you to is the kind of work (a) that you need most to do and (b) that the world most needs to have done. If you really get a kick out of your work, you've presumably met regulation (a). But if your work is writing TV deodorant commercials, the chances are you've missed regulation (b). On the other hand, if your work is being a doctor in a leper colony—you've probably met regulation (b), but if you're bored and depressed by it, the chances are you have not only bypassed (a) but probably aren't helping your patients much either.

Buechner concludes, "The place God calls you to is the place where your deep gladness and the world's deep hunger meet." There is no shortage of needs to which a Christian can respond. But I'm wondering if the church is clearly articulating those needs. If the needs were clearly defined, surely more of us would immediately arise and say: "Here am I, send me!"

In a paper from the National Council of Churches Professional Church Leadership "Future of Ministry" project, Peggy Shriver asks the question: "With some loss of prestige, security, and community standing in an increasingly diverse society and a somewhat weakened church structure, with relatively low pay and high educational costs, with needs in society that make one's head swim—why would any sensible human being enter the ministry today?"

Good question! At a local high school career night, I noticed that no one ever thought to present the option of the ministry. There were booths for the military, medical professions, banking and computer-related fields, but nothing related to ministry. Is ministry so out of the question or so obviously unattractive that no one ever gives it a thought? If so, that marks a real change in our society. Ministry used to hold a very high status in our culture. The major universities in the United States were founded for the training of clergy.

How is the office of the ministry perceived by the wider culture these days? Do people think first of certain televangelists embroiled in scandal? Can you name one nationally prominent clergyperson for whom there is general regard? What has fostered this demise in the status of the clergy?

Back to the question as to why anyone would enter the ministry today— Shriver attempts to answer her own question:

> One enters ministry for the same reasons persons down through the ages have served the church—for the love of God and humanity. Prestige, money, security, standing and educational elitism have never been the intended goals of ministry. . . . [Ministers] only need the skillful training and blessing of the church. They may feel a special calling to work among people with unique needs or cultures. They may bring training from other disciplines to enrich their ministry, or enlist the human resource skills of others in caring collaboration. Their hands may speak better than their tongues, or their tongues better than their hands the forgiving love of Jesus. God is already at work in them, and through them God indeed does not abandon us.

Jesus told his disciples, "The harvest is plentiful, but the laborers are few." That is true today as well. But just as true today as then are the great needs in our world that God would have us address with compassion.

"Then Jesus summoned his twelve disciples and gave them authority . . . " (Matt. 10:1). It was Jesus' compassion that precipitated the calling of the twelve, but once they were called, Jesus sensed the need to authorize them for service.

Many levels of authorization exist in any given church structure. It has never been enough for a person simply to announce independently that he or she has experienced a call from God. The church has had to test these calls for authenticity. That has frequently been a difficult experience for the church, and often it hasn't been done well. But an authentic call can be tested.

In your denomination's book of worship you will find any number of commissioning services. These represent the various ways the church grants authority to people called for specific tasks. We commission teachers, missionaries, evangelists, and preachers and, sometimes, volunteers, deacons, work campers, and others.

At our baptism we all experience the call to ministry that comes from Christ. Special forms of that ministry are then called forth from the church. The call to be disciples is not an endurance test or an admission exam. It is not a prerequisite for a place in the church or the family of God. The call to discipleship is the impulsive response of compassion for God's world. Compassion drives us to the crossroads of our deepest gladness and the world's deep hunger.

Discussion and Action

1. Share your meaning for the word *compassion.*
2. Do you think compassion is a natural inclination? Respond to the suggestion that compassion "is not a natural response."
3. What do you suppose were the concerns of the people who came to Jesus?
4. What are the great needs in the world today to which God calls us to respond?
5. Thinking about your own work, how do you (and it) measure up to Buechner's two-part rule?
6. How do people today perceive the ministry as a profession? Why would you encourage anyone to go into the ministry?
7. How does your church authorize Christian servants?
8. Close your study of *When God Calls* by singing (or reading together) Thomas Townsend's hymn "Called by Christ" (to the tune Cwm Rhondda, "God of Grace and God of Glory").

> Called by Christ from life with narrow meaning,
>> Called to live by God possessed.
> Claimed to know God's love, all reconciling,
>> Claimed to be that love, expressed.
> This is my purpose, God, I thank Thee.
>> Use my life through Christ my Lord.
>> Use my life through Christ my Lord.

Suggestions for Sharing and Prayer

During your study of *When God Calls*, you will journey through some of the classic spiritual disciplines. Consider having each member of the group keep a journal of prayer and reflection throughout the ten weeks. Share with one another from your journals during group meetings.

Below you'll find suggestions for forms of prayer that may be new to you. As you use these different forms of prayer, you will no doubt find your prayer experience with God deepened.

In the scriptures people are called by God out of the ordinariness of their lives, and they respond out of their openness to receive God's call. By practicing the spiritual disciplines—solitude, silence, prayer, meditation, worship, fasting, submission, Bible study, and celebration—we can receive God's call more clearly. Through these disciplines, may you discover numerous creative ways of enriching your prayer life.

This section was written by Harriet Finney and Suzanne DeMoss Brown, who have been members of the People of the Covenant development team. We hope these suggestions will spark your own ideas and help you to be more open and attentive to God's call in your lives.

1. God Calls Abraham: *The Discipline of Journaling*

❑ Abram was blessed by God at the time of his call. What blessings have you received through God's call in your life? How have you been a blessing to others? If you are too modest to say, take turns naming ways group members have blessed others. Make sure everyone is mentioned.

❑ Each sharing session will focus on a classical spiritual discipline. Keep a journal for prayer and reflection during these weeks. A journal is a notebook in which to record your personal prayers, thoughts, and reflections. Writing prayers, poems, hymns, and notes, and attaching clippings that include art work and other items meaningful in your prayer life give a reflection of your personal spiritual journey.

❑ Begin your journaling by . . .
a. trying a new form of prayer during these ten weeks, such as singing,

dancing or creative movement, using musical instruments, writing, creating art work, focusing on God's creation.

b. finding a place to focus on God apart from the clutter and "busyness" of our daily lives. Spend some time imagining your life without schedules, noise, telephones, and television.

c. sharing your thoughts from your journal writings with the group as you choose.

❑ Pray together, using prayers of praise, thanksgiving, and intercession.

2. Gods Calls Moses: *The Discipline of Solitude*

❑ Share with the group your experience of journaling and prayer during the week. How is it going for you? Is it difficult? What discoveries have you made this week as you wrote in your journal?

❑ Recall a "holy ground" event in your life. How did that moment of solitude, of meeting God, serve you? How has it served God?

❑ Tell about a time you were completely alone. How comfortable are you with solitude? How near to God do you feel in solitude?

❑ If possible, turn your chairs to face outward. Take a few moments to be alone in the presence of God. Reflect on your baptism and its meaning for you. Pass a bowl of water so that those who wish to may lightly sprinkle drops of water on their faces as they experience God's presence anew in life. Record your reflections in your journal.

❑ Learn to sing the hymn, "Sing, Child of God" (p. 54).

❑ Close your sharing time with the hymn "There Is a Place of Quiet Rest" (p. 55), and conclude with spoken prayers.

❑ Covenant with each other to spend time in solitude this coming week.

3. God Calls Samuel and Hannah: *The Discipline of Silence*

❑ Share your experiences of solitude during the week, including both the positive and the negative.

❑ Silently reflect: How was I, as a child, dedicated to God? Who dedicated me? What does this mean for me today?

❏ Respond to this question, How do I hear God's call (e.g., in scripture, in nature, in people)? Instead of sharing verbally, silently write your responses on posted newsprint as you reflect on the question.

❏ Covenant that in the coming week you will be open to God's presence in silence, perhaps through your dreams, while walking out-of-doors, or in hearing a robin's call. Record your experiences in your journal.

❏ Read the words of the hymn, "O God, in Restless Living" (p. 56). Sing them at intervals between silent prayers.

❏ Sing together "I Can Hear My Savior Calling" or another hymn about responding to God's call. Follow this with spoken prayers of praise and thanksgiving.

4. God Calls Ruth: *The Discipline of Fasting*

❏ Share anything you "heard" as you reflected in silence during the week.

❏ It is not recorded that Ruth had a clear call from God to travel with Naomi. She did it out of a natural concern for others. Like the young man who shovels snow for an elderly neighbor, or the grandmother who responds to her granddaughter's needs by mending clothes or helping prepare a holiday meal, we all want to help out of love. Name some of the ordinary ways people around you are responding to the needs around them.

❏ As you think about fasting, share experiences members of your group have had with fasting. Generally, we think of fasting as depriving oneself of food. A better understanding of fasting is that we gain insight and sharpen our focus on God by going without food. Other ways of fasting might include giving up television or excessive use of the telephone, or giving up overwork to find balance in life and allow time to focus on God.

❏ Think for a moment about the things from which you need to fast. Tell the group. Decide in what way you will fast during the coming week. Record your experiences with fasting in your journal.

❏ Pray "fasting-style" prayers: sit in silence and then speak brief prayers, using one word or a simple phrase. Close by praying together the Lord's Prayer.

5. God Calls David: *The Discipline of Prayer*

❑ Tell about your fast during the week. How did it go? What insight did you gain through it?

❑ What is prayer to you? How do you usually pray? Do you more often pray, "Speak, Lord, your servant is listening," or "Listen, Lord, your servant is speaking"? Think of biblical examples of both.

❑ Tell about your prayer life as a child, a youth, and an adult. How have your prayers changed over time?

❑ As you pray together, include moments of silent prayer, listening for what God speaks to you. Close by singing: Into my heart, into my heart/ come into my heart, Lord Jesus/ come in today, come in to stay/ come into my heart, Lord Jesus.

❑ Name things you are thankful for, angry about, or confused about. Then name people and issues you want to bring to God in intercession. Have two people say prayers of thanksgiving and intercession, speaking your shared prayers.

❑ Be creative. Help each other think of ways to pray other than speaking. How can hiking, singing, gardening, and writing be prayers?

❑ During your personal prayer time this week, give special attention to listening as well as speaking. Reflect on the areas of your life in need of healing (relationships, physical needs, spiritual dis-ease). Record these prayer experiences.

6. God Calls Jeremiah: *The Discipline of Meditation*

❑ Share from your journal entries some of your experiences of personal prayer and some of the needs for healing in your life. Pray an invocation prayer to invite God into your midst. Incorporate the needs and desires of the group into the prayer.

❑ Jeremiah's response to God was, "I am too young." How do you experience God's call in people of all ages (young children, teenagers, young and older adults)? Who in your group or congregation needs a call from you to confirm what God may be saying to him or her? Commit yourselves to calling out the gifts of others.

❑ Meditation is focusing on scripture, a hymn, a beautiful flower or sunset, and seeing God. In your prayer time this week, meditate on something that draws your mind toward God. Write your thoughts, feelings, and reflections in your journal.

❑ Name a favorite scripture. Meditate on the group's favorite verses for five minutes and reflect your thoughts aloud to the group.

❑ Share in a meditative closing worship, using the words of God's call to Jeremiah and words from Isaiah 43:1-7. Read the words of the hymn "Here I Am, Lord" in a reflective, prayerful way (p. 57). Then sing the hymn.

❑ Wander around the place you are meeting. Find an object that symbol-izes God's creation—a plant, a shell, a rock. Focus on your object for one minute. Then pass your object to the right and meditate on creation for one more minute. Keep objects circulating until everyone has seen all objects. Share any reflections aloud.

7. God Calls Isaiah: *The Discipline of Worship*

❑ Share your journal entries from your meditation times. How has meditation helped you focus on God? How does meditation inspire you to respond to God?

❑ Describe a worship service that has been especially meaningful to you. Did you sense God's call at the time? What do you usually expect when you participate in worship? Is there a possibility of seraphs? Is there room for the Spirit of God to fill the room?

❑ Name the elements of a worship. What must be done to have true worship? Prepare a 5- to 15-minute worship plan you could follow each day in the coming week.

❑ Pay special attention in worship at church. At what points are you most engaged? If you could worship, what scriptures, readings, and hymns would you use? What would you like to preach about?

❑ Share with each other some of your favorite hymns of praise, thanks-giving, and intercession. Sing some of these as you close your time of sharing and prayer.

8. God Calls Mary: *The Discipline of Submission*

❑ How did corporate worship come alive for you this week? What would make worship more meaningful for you each week?

❑ When the angel told Mary she would give birth to Jesus, Mary responded first with the question "How can this be?" then with the words "Let it be!" Tell about a time you feel you submitted to the will of God, even when it was not easy.

❑ In prayer, offer up to God the ways you think you are in control of your life (e.g., money, health, parenting). Name them aloud. Then say sentence prayers asking for the courage to let go of control and help in submitting yourself to God's will. Write some of these sentence prayers in your journal, and use them in your spiritual discipline this coming week.

❑ How easy or hard is it to be obedient to Jesus? Name some rewards of obedience. Who has achieved these rewards? Write a confessional prayer in your journal on obedience.

❑ Sing together the hymn "Take My Life" (p. 59), and pray sentence prayers of praise, thanksgiving, and intercession.

9. God Calls Paul and Ananias: *The Discipline of Bible Study*

❑ Share some of your reflections on obedience from your journal. How much like Mary are you?

❑ God called Paul in a very dramatic way to get his attention. Tell how God has gotten your attention. How did you respond?

❑ God's call to Ananias demanded great faith and courage. Make a litany together. List all the things God has called you to do that you don't want to do. Read them aloud together. Between each one say, "God, give us courage."

❑ Most of us have used rather traditional ways to study the Bible in Sunday school, both in small groups and in personal devotions. Choose one of the following ways to study Acts 9:1-19:
a. Each person reads the passage aloud, inserting his or her name in place of Saul's. Does this method bring more meaning out of the text for you? How?

b. Work together as a group, rewriting the passage as if it were happening today. What did you learn about the text?

❏ Look in study Bibles, single-volume commentaries, or Bible dictionaries for more information about Paul. After reading for a few minutes, work together to tell the life story of Paul.

❏ During the week study the scripture for session 10, using more than one method (e.g., read the scripture aloud; rewrite the text, putting yourself into Matthew 9:35—10:4; thoughtfully pray the words of the text). Note in your journal your responses to your study.

❏ Offer prayers of praise, thanksgiving, and intercession from the scriptures, such as the Psalms of praise and thanksgiving, the Lord's Prayer, or Mary's Song (Luke 1:46-55).

10. God Calls Disciples: *The Discipline of Celebration*

❏ Share some thoughts on Bible study from your journal. How do you get the most out of your Bible? How easy or difficult is Bible study for you?

❏ Share with the group how it has been for you to intentionally practice some of the spiritual disciplines. This week enjoy the discipline of celebration by choosing one of the following activities:

a. Paint, draw, or sculpt. Art is a way to respond to God's call by involving more than just our minds. This becomes an expression of the "mystery of life" as it emerges! After finishing your creation, look at it from all angles; discover what it says or means. Then title it, perhaps using a scripture or words from a hymn. Add your name and date.

b. Bombard with gifts. Sit in a circle and name the gifts of each person in your group. Have one person write down each person's gifts as they are named. Spend one or two minutes on each person while he or she receives your verbal gifts. Give the person their written list of gifts.

c. Eat together. Sharing a meal is a common discipline of the church community. Jesus commanded that we remember him in the breaking of bread.

d. Sing. Celebrate with your favorite hymns and songs of faith.

e. Encourage each other. Pass journals around the room. Write an encouraging message or greeting in each person's journal, emphasizing God's call and our response.

❑ Close your sharing and prayer time, using one or several of the following:
a. Pray for one another by name.
b. Read together the litany "Called to Serve God," by April Yamasaki (p. 50).
c. Sing together a hymn of calling and commitment. In addition to hymns used in the study, the following are suggested: "Jesus Calls Us," "I Can Hear My Savior Calling," or "Have Thine Own Way, Lord."

General Sharing and Prayer Resources

Forming a Covenant Group

Covenant Expectations
Covenant-making is significant throughout the biblical story. God made covenants with Noah, Abraham, and Moses. Jeremiah spoke about God making a covenant with the people, "written on the heart." In the New Testament, Jesus was identified as the mediator of the New Covenant, and the early believers lived out of covenant relationships. Throughout history people have lived in covenant relationship with God and within community.

Christians today also covenant with God and make commitments to each other. Such covenants help believers live out their faith. God's empowerment comes to them as they gather in covenant communities to pray and study, share and receive, reflect and act.

People of the Covenant is a program that is anchored in this covenantal history of God's people. It is a network of covenantal relationships. Denominations, districts or regions, congregations, small groups, and individuals all make covenants. Covenant group members commit themselves to the mission statement, seeking to become more . . .

—biblically informed so they better understand the revelation of God;
—globally aware so they know themselves to be better connected with all of God's world;
—relationally sensitive to God, self, and others.

The Burlap Cross Symbol
The imperfections of the burlap cross, its rough texture and unrefined fabric, the interweaving of threads, the uniqueness of each strand, are elements that are present within the covenant group. The people in the groups are imperfect, unpolished, interrelated with each other, yet still unique beings.

The shape that this collection of imperfect threads creates is the cross, symbolizing for all Christians the resurrection and presence of Christ our Savior. A covenant group is something akin to this burlap cross. It unites common, ordinary people and sends them out again in all directions to be in the world.

A Litany: Called to Serve God

Listen to the silence. Can you hear the voice of God? Closer than the sound of our own breathing, more insistent than the beat of our own hearts, God calls us. Listen.
(Read Matthew 6:19-24)

Our lives are crowded with many voices.

The marketplace calls us to set our sights on its material goods.

The workplace calls us to climb its ladder of success.

The community calls us to devote ourselves to social service.

The church calls us to support its worship and mission activities.

The home circle calls us to commit ourselves to family and friends.

But Jesus calls us to love and serve God above all these things.

"Do not lay up . . . treasures on earth . . . but lay up for yourselves treasure in heaven . . . . For where your treasure is, there will your heart be also."

Do not be concerned about acquiring the temporary pleasures and possessions of this world . . . but value the life and work of the kingdom of God, for whatever stands at the center of your life will order your priorities. . . .

"No one can serve two masters; for either he will hate the one and love the other, or be devoted to the one and despise the other."

No one can give a single-minded commitment to two different things To give ourselves wholeheartedly to God, we must give up all others.

"You cannot serve God and mammon."

We cannot give wholehearted devotion to both God and money.

We cannot give wholehearted devotion to both God and our own prestige and reputation.

Even our work in the community, the church, and among family and friends must be set in relation to God, for even a good work can become a false master and a false god.

But there is one God, whose face we seek.

There is one God, whose voice we long to hear. Listen!

Our God, as we try to sort out the many voices in our world, keep us single-minded in our commitment to you. Order our priorities according to your will, we pray. Amen.

From *Where Two Are Gathered*, by April Yamasaki, © 1988 Brethren Press

Prayer of Praise
Holy Spirit . . .
You are the cause of all movement;
You are the breath of all creatures;
You are the salve that purifies our souls;
You are the ointment that heals our wounds;
You are the fire that warms our hearts;
You are the light that guides our feet.
Let all the world praise you.
—Hippolytus (190-236)

Prayers of Submission and Dedication

Lord, I freely yield to You all my liberty.
Take my memory, my intellect, and my entire will.
You have given me everything I am or have;
I give it all back to you to stand under your will alone.
Your love and Your grace are enough for me,
I ask for nothing more.
—St. Ignatius of Loyola (1491-1556)

O eternal God,
Turn us into the arms and hands,
The legs and feet
Of your beloved Son, Jesus.
You gave birth to him in heaven
Before the creation of the earth.
You gave birth to us on earth,
To become his living body.
Make us worthy to be his limbs,
And so worthy to share
In his eternal bliss.

> —Hildegard of Bingen

I am yours, you made me.
I am yours, you called me.
I am yours, you saved me.
I am yours, you loved me.
I will never leave your presence.

> —Teresa of Avila (1515-1582)

A Promise of Guidance

When you call upon me and come and pray to me,
I will hear you.
When you search for me, you will find me;
if you seek me with all your heart,
I will let you find me, says the LORD,
and I will restore your fortunes
and gather you from all the nations and all the places
where I have driven you, says the LORD,
and I will bring you back to the place
from which I sent you into exile.

> —Jeremiah 29:12-14

On the Call to Compassion

It seems clear to me
    that in some way we must unite
        our wills with God's will.
But it is in the effects and
    deeds following afterwards

that one discerns the true
value of prayer.
There is no better crucible for
testing prayer than compassion.
—Teresa of Avila (1515-1582)

On Enablement to Discern
You are a fire,
ever burning and never consumed.
You consume in your heart all the self-love within my soul,
taking away all coldness.
You are a light,
ever shining and never fainting.
You drive away all the darkness within my heart,
enabling me to see your glorious truth.
—Catherine of Siena (1447-1510)

An Affirmation of Faith
Though the fig tree does not blossom,
and no fruit is on the vines;
though the produce of the olive fails and the fields yield no food;
though the flock is cut off from the fold
and there is no herd in the stalls,
yet I will rejoice in the LORD;
I will exult in the God of my salvation.
—Habakkuk 3:17-18

A Response to Call
A disturber of the peace am I? Yes indeed, of my own peace. Do you call
this disturbing the peace that instead of spending my time in frivolous
amusements I have visited the plague infested and carried out the dead? I
have visited those in prison and under sentence of death. Often for three days
and three nights I have neither eaten nor slept. I have never mounted the
pulpit, but I have done more than any minister in visiting those in misery. Is
this disturbing the peace of the church?
—Katherine Zell (author and hymn writer, 1497-1562)

Sing, Child of God

1 Sing, child of God, to a wea - ry __ world; Sing of your
2 Sing, child of God, to a world in des - pair; Sing from your

faith, let its joy be un - furled. Sing, child of God, to a
be - ing to show that you care. Sing, child of God, what you

wea - ry __ world; Sing, child of God, sing. ___
feel must be told. Sing, child of God, sing. ___

Sing with your love, toss it out on the air; Sing with your
Sing with com - pas - sion that heart - break may cease; Sing from your

hope, it's the lan - guage of prayer. Sing, child of God, to a
pain, and in shar - ing gain peace. Sing, child of God, Sing, __

wea - ry __ world. Sing, child of God, sing. ___
share, and re - joice. Sing, child of God, sing. ___

Text and music: Lena Willoughby
Arranger: Leonard Blickenstaff
Copyright © 1979 Brethren Press

There Is a Place of Quiet Rest

1 There is a place of qui - et rest, Near to the heart of God,
2 There is a place of com - fort sweet, Near to the heart of God,
3 There is a place of full re - lease, Near to the heart of God,

A place where sin can - not mo - lest, Near to the heart of God.
A place where we our Sav - iour meet, Near to the heart of God.
A place where all is joy and peace, Near to the heart of God.

O Je - sus, blest Re - deem - er, Sent from the heart of God,

Hold us, who wait be - fore Thee, Near to the heart of God.

Text and music: Cleland B. McAfee, 1866-1944

O God, in Restless Living

1 O God, in rest - less liv - ing we lose our spir - it's peace.
2 Teach us, be - yond our striv - ing, the rich re - wards of rest.
3 Re - cep - tive make our spir - its, our need is to be still.
4 We grow not wise by strug - gling, we gain but things by strain.

Calm our un - wise con - fu - sion, bid thou our clam - or cease.
Who does not live se - rene - ly is nev - er deep - ly bless'd.
As dawn fades flick - 'ring can - dle so dim our anx - ious will.
We cease to wa - ter gar - dens, when comes thy plen - teous rain.

Let anx - ious hearts grow qui - et, like pools at eve - ning still,
O tran - quil, ra - diant Sun - light, bring thou our lives to flow'r,
Re - veal thy ra - diance through us, thine am - ple strength re - lease.
O, beau - ti - fy our spir - its in rest - ful - ness from strife,

till thy re - flect - ed heav - ens all our spir - its fill.
less wea - ried with our ef - fort, more a - ware of pow'r.
Not ours, but thine the tri - umph in the pow'r of peace.
en - rich our souls in se - cret with a - bun - dant life.

Text: Harry Emerson Fosdick, 1878-1969
Music: Edward F. Rimbault, 1816-1876

Here I Am, Lord

1. I, the Lord of sea and sky,	2. I. the Lord of snow and rain,	3. I, the Lord of wind and flame,
I have heard my people cry,	I have borne my people's pain.	I will tend the poor and lame.
All who dwell in dark and sin	I have wept for love of them.	I will set a feast for them.
my hand will save.	They turn away.	My hand will save.
I who made the stars of night,	I will break their hearts of stone,	Finest bread will I provide,
I will make their darkness bright.	give them hearts for love alone.	till their hearts be satisfied.
Who will bear my light to them?	I will speak my word to them.	I will give my life to them.
Whom shall I send?	Whom shall I send?	Whom shall I send?
(Refrain)	(Refrain)	(Refrain)

Text: based on Isaiah 6 by Daniel L. Schutte
Music: Daniel L. Schutte. Arranged by Michael Pope, S.J. and John Weissrock

Let All Mortal Flesh Keep Silence

Unison

1 Let all mor - tal flesh keep si - lence, and with fear and
2 King of kings, yet born of Ma - ry, as of old on
3 Rank on rank the host of heav - en spreads its van - guard
4 At his feet the six - winged ser - aph, cher - u - bim with

trem - bling stand. Pon - der noth - ing earth - ly mind - ed,
earth he stood, Lord of lords in hu - man ves - ture,
on the way, as the Light of light, de - scend - eth
sleep - less eye, veil their fac - es to the Pres - ence,

for with bless - ing in his hand Christ our God to earth de -
in the bod - y and the blood, he will give to all the
from the realms of end - less day, that the pow'rs of hell may
as with cease - less voice they cry, "Al - le - lu - ia! Al - le -

scend - eth, our full hom - age to de - mand.
faith - ful, his own self for heav'n - ly food.
van - ish, as the dark - ness clears a - way.
lu - ia! Al - le - lu - ia, Lord Most High!"

Text: *Liturgy of St. James of Jerusalem*, 5th c.
Music: French carol, 1860

Take My Life

1 Take my life and let it be Con - se - crat - ed, Lord, to
2 Take my hands and let them move At the im - pulse of Thy
3 Take my voice and let me sing Al - ways, on - ly, for my
4 Take my sil - ver and my gold; Not a mite would I with -
5 Take my love; my Lord, I pour At Thy feet its treas - ure

1 Thee. Take my mo - ments and my days, Let them flow in
2 love. Take my feet and let them be Swift and beau - ti -
3 King. Take my lips and let them be Filled with mes - sag -
4 hold. Take my in - tel - lect, and use Ev - 'ry pow'r as
5 store. Take my - self, and I will be Ev - er, on - ly,

1 cease - less praise, Let them flow in cease - less praise.
2 ful for Thee, Swift and beau - ti - ful for Thee.
3 es from Thee, Filled with mes - sag - es from Thee.
4 Thou shalt choose, Ev - 'ry pow'r as Thou shalt choose.
5 all for Thee, Ev - er, on - ly, all for Thee. A - men.

Text: Frances R. Havergal, 1836-1879
Music: H. A. César Malan, 1787-1864

Other Covenant Bible Studies

To place an order, call Brethren Press toll-free Monday through Friday, 8 A.M. to 4 P.M., at **800-441-3712** or fax an order to **800-667-8188** twenty-four hours a day. Shipping and handling will be added to each order. For a full description of each title, ask for a free catalog of these and other Brethren Press titles.

Visa and MasterCard accepted. Prices subject to change.

Brethren Press® • *faithQuest*® • 1451 Dundee Ave., Elgin, IL 60120-1694
800-441-3712 (orders) • 800-667-8188